EAST END & DOCKLANDS

In the West India Dock, tower blocks to the left, enterprise zone construction centre.

EAST END & DOCKLANDS

William J. Fishman
Nicholas Breach
John M. Hall

Duckworth

First published in 1990 by
Gerald Duckworth & Co. Ltd.
The Old Piano Factory
43 Gloucester Crescent, London NW1

ISBN 0 7156 2343 5

British Library Cataloguing in Publication Data

British Library Cataloguing in Publication data
Fishman, William J. (William Jack)
   East End & Docklands.
   1. England, history. East End & Docklands
   I. Title   II. Breach, Nicholas   III. Hall, John M. (John Martin), *1946-*
942.15

ISBN 0-7156-2343-5

Filmset and printed in Great Britain by
BAS Printers Limited, Over Wallop, Hampshire

CONTENTS

Photographs and captions by Nicholas Breach

Across the river from Rotherhithe to the Wapping shore.

INTRODUCTION

by Nicholas Breach

The first edition of *The Streets of East London* came out in 1979, and the photographs of the East End as it then was were taken in 1977 and 1978. Ten years on we look again at what has changed and what has remained the same. In *Streets of East London* we contrasted periods separated by nearly a century, and included archival pictures from the 1880s and 1890s: but now many shots of the 1970s have themselves become the archive.

So what has happened? In Spitalfields at least lessons have been learnt and some imaginative decisions have been made. The new health centre at the Osborn Street end of Brick Lane may not be to everyone's aesthetic taste, but in social terms it represents a solid advance (not least when we remember what was there before, which was nothing). New development in the Flower & Dean and Thrawl Street areas acknowledges the general dislike of tower-block and deck-access flats and offers instead traditional two-storey homes. Hawksmoor's Christ Church is being restored, and so, through the medium of gentrification, is Fournier Street. But the pressure on housing stock in East London as a whole continues to be acute, and the recent shift towards the private sector has done nothing for those most in need. For the poor are always with us, and the Providence Row night shelter in Crispin Street, witness to more than a hundred years of deprivation, still does capacity business.

In 1979 we chose to exclude dockland from our brief, references to the strike of 1889 and the general strike of 1926 apart. The docks, by the end of the seventies, were dead. I remember the George V dock in Silvertown one autumn afternoon in 1977: in the whole of that melancholy expanse of water a solitary Malaysian ship was tied up. Two shots of the London Docks, taken about the same time but never used, are reproduced here (see pp. 68 & 69). They are utterly desolate.

The docks could not have remained as they were, a sad and mouldering monument to a once great industry. Something had to be done: that is not at issue.

But what has been done is.

Because here was a single opportunity for London as great as any since the immediate post-war years. The memory of the mistakes made then, notably the abandonment of conventional housing for the detested high rise, should have been enough to concentrate anyone's mind. Yet design in the new docklands, whether domestic or commercial, has been at best depressingly uninventive and at worst wildly egocentric. We are given acres of high priced identikit estates, lacking the remotest spirit of community, and aimed exclusively at the upwardly mobile (during those halcyon days when it seemed that property would appreciate forever it was the declared intention of many to take a quick profit and get back to Chelsea or Fulham as soon as possible). The interests of the original residents, in the enterprise zone especially, have been neglected, often scandalously; viable local businesses have been, and are still being displaced, and house prices are hopeless. For local people employment opportunities within the zone are pathetically few, no more than ten per cent of the whole. They are victims of the draconian powers vested in the London Docklands Development Corporation: and it is private gain, not public good, that has dictated policy.

Their pickings, whose bones?

Greenwich, across the water from the Isle of Dogs, may be more fortunate. Though the authorities there have their own riverside to develop they sensibly regard the story of docklands as a cautionary tale, and have made it plain that they will consult everyone concerned before any plans are drawn up or decisions made. High rise, in any case, is out: but Greenwich will still have to look at Canary Wharf.

Monetarism has set its mark upon docklands as it has upon so much in the last decade. We have been lectured repeatedly about the values and entrepreneurial skills of the last century, so the government, recently engaged in the cynical sell-off of a vital public asset, water, might find of interest the views of a Victorian doctor, Hector Gavin, who was much concerned with the public health issues of his day. In 1848 he published a book called *Sanitary Ramblings* in which he documented in detail the lamentable conditions then suffered by the wretched inhabitants of Bethnal Green. In the course of it he wrote: 'It is necessary however to observe, that the price at which water is supplied, on the present highly objectionable plan, is excessively high, and that water, forming one of the main necessaries of life, being more important even than food, should be provided by the public, to the public; on the most economical terms possible, and that no principle of justice can countenance the exorbitant prices now charged for water . . . when it has been abundantly proved, that a sufficient supply of pure water at a very cheap rate can readily be obtained.'

A country which ignores its history may be forced to relive it. Is this where we all came in?

EAST END

by William J. Fishman

In general, changes in Whitechapel and its environs over the last ten years appear dramatic.

The Rothschild Dwellings and its sister complex between once unsalubrious Lolesworth and Flower & Dean Street have vanished. They have been replaced by low, two-storeyed semi-detached cottages enclosed within a modern all-purpose housing estate – thanks to Toynbee Hall, which has itself expanded its original settlement to include new housing and offices. At the southern end of Brick Lane, the erstwhile waste land has been filled by colourful Bangladeshi stores at the ground level of low-rise apartment blocks. Fashion Street, within its multi-variety of shops and cottage-based workshops, solidly maintains its past.

One block to the north, running parallel to it, lies historic Fournier Street with its ancient façades, of early eighteenth-century vintage, restored to their period style or, in parts, remodelled. The houses have reverted to homes for an invading middle class, turning the clock back to their origins – as the once elegant houses of thrusting Huguenot entrepreneurs. At the junction of Fournier Street and Brick Lane L'Eglise Neuve (built in 1743) still stands. From Huguenot Church it has been transformed by turns into Methodist Chapel (1808), Jewish Synagogue (1897) and finally Great Mosque.

But what has become of those Bengali Muslim worshippers we had observed only two years before in that same Fournier Street, bending over machines in the sweatshops? The old Georgian houses are saved, but little seems to have been done to find alternative housing for the displaced immigrant. It is a sort of action-replay of a century ago, when the demolition of mass rookeries in congested slums around the Hawksmoor Church to make way for Commercial Street, with little plan for rehousing the poor, led to homelessness and more pressure on reduced accommodation. The main result was the overcrowding of neighbouring streets and alleyways with an accompanying increase in disease and crime. Will the authorities ever learn!

The ancient fruit and flower market (established by Royal Charter in the 1680s) is threatened with closure and similar problems are inevitable. Compulsory plans for redevelopment to provide 1·9 million square feet of offices and shops plus *some* public and private housing to replace the 12-acre Spitalfields market offer little hope that homes will be built for local folk. We can only concur with Dan Cruickshank's assumption, optimistic though it is, that 'if the tendency to scale down community benefits emerges in negotiation, then it must be stopped by DoE intervention!'* Otherwise Nicholas Breach's prognosis of failure will prove true.

Yet much of the old and familiar is still in place: the three

*'Towering problems in Hawksmoor's backyard' in the *Independent*, 6 December 1989.

A Fournier Street courtyard.

main brewery sites – Trumans, Brick Lane, the Albion brewery, Whitechapel, and Charringtons; the homeless and transient still sprawling in Itchy Park (when open), while the nearby Crypt, at the side of the great Christ Church, continues to cleanse and clothe them; the Brune Street Soup Kitchen for the Jewish Poor (opened in 1902) offering parcels free at High Holydays for the old and needy; the equally compassionate Sisters of Mercy at the Providence Row Night Refuge in Crispin Street keeping ever-open house to feed and shelter the lonely and the desperate.

Toynbee Hall, under a traditionally enterprising Warden, has embarked on new social ventures complementing the old. The Whitechapel Art Gallery, brainchild of the Barnetts, continues to flourish, its exhibitions commanding national attention, while two hundred yards eastward across the Whitechapel Road the ancient Whitechapel Bell Foundry (founded in 1570) still casts its bells for an international market. One can still enter the Angel Alley courtyard by the side of the Art Gallery where Martha Turner, arguably the first of the Ripper victims, was last seen alive, and where the Freedom Press (conceived by Prince Kropotkin in 1886), still stands, manned by its kindly, colourful eccentrics who propagate, and live out, their Libertarian creed. Old Jack still haunts this precinct. For as long as those few cobbled alleyways and leprous-walled culs-de-sac along the Cockney mile remain, so also will Whitechapel sustain its Victorian image as a 'city of dreadful night'.

At the eastern corner of Fieldgate Street astride the main road stands another great mosque, and from the Tower of Darkness a *muezzin* calls the new faithful to prayer. But the

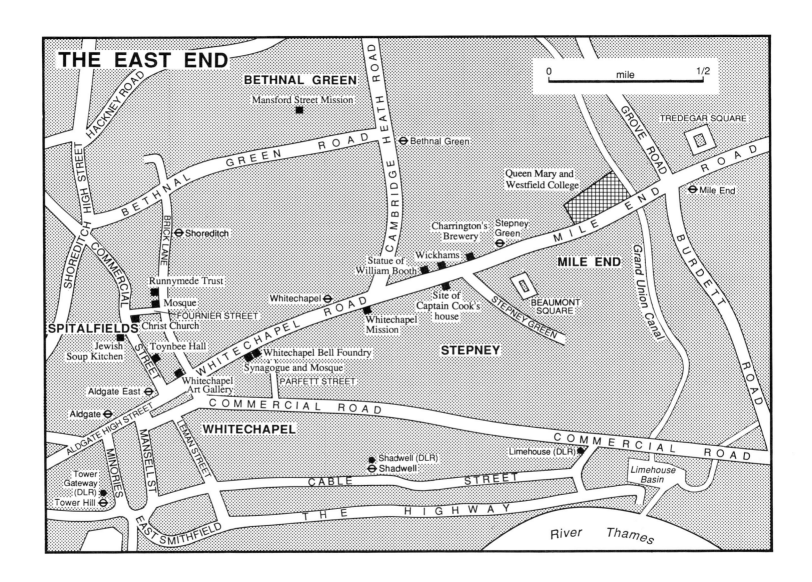

THE EAST END

BETHNAL GREEN

Mansford Street Mission

0   mile   1/2

TREDEGAR SQUARE

⊖ Bethnal Green

HACKNEY ROAD

SHOREDITCH HIGH STREET

BETHNAL GREEN ROAD

CAMBRIDGE HEATH ROAD

GROVE ROAD

ROAD

⊖ Mile End

Queen Mary and
Westfield College

COMMERCIAL

BRICK LANE

⊖ Shoreditch

Charrington's
Brewery

Stepney
Green
⊖

MILE END ROAD

MILE END

BURDETT ROAD

Wickhams

Grand Union Canal

Runnymede Trust

Statue of
William Booth

Whitechapel ⊖

Site of
Captain Cook's
house

BEAUMONT
SQUARE

Mosque

FOURNIER STREET

Christ Church

Whitechapel
Mission

STEPNEY GREEN

SPITALFIELDS

WHITECHAPEL ROAD

STEPNEY

Jewish
Soup Kitchen

Toynbee Hall

Whitechapel Bell Foundry

Synagogue and Mosque

STREET

Whitechapel
Art Gallery

PARFETT STREET

Aldgate East ⊖

COMMERCIAL ROAD

Aldgate ⊖

ALDGATE HIGH STREET

LEMAN STREET

WHITECHAPEL

COMMERCIAL ROAD

MANSELL ST

Shadwell (DLR)
⊖ Shadwell

Limehouse (DLR)

Tower
Gateway
(DLR)

MINORIES

Limehouse
Basin

Tower Hill ⊖

CABLE

STREET

EAST SMITHFIELD

THE   HIGHWAY

River   Thames

continuity of history is there. Adjoining the rear of the mosque is the Fieldgate Street Synagogue (consecrated in 1899) where the last of the old faithful – a rump of ageing Jews – muster to recite passages from the Talmud. Side by side the two faiths worship in perfect amity: an act of tolerance that should not be lost on their co-religionists elsewhere.

Further eastwards by the side of the London Hospital, Cavell Street makes its way south into Ford Square to reveal stark contrasts in class habitations. The same two-storeyed cottages are sharply divided into noticeably diminishing run-down rented accommodation alongside recently ultra-modernised homes divided into private apartments for sale. In 1978 estate agents' prices for these were: a one-bedroomed apartment £72,000, two-bedroomed £76,000 and three-bedroomed £103,000 – all obviously beyond the pockets of the local Bangladeshi. Again, another middle-class incursion into a once predominantly working-class enclave forcing an exodus of its old inhabitants to – where?

But in response to the incoming homeless and transient unemployed, vastly increased in numbers during the last decade (and dramatically in the last two years!) there are the traditional dedicated 'saints': men and women drawn to the East End to succour, not only the desperately poor, but the inadequates, the feckless and a growing band of the mentally unstable, discharged from institutions into government-defined 'community care'.

Thus the warm, ebullient Rev. Peter Jennings, Methodist minister to the Whitechapel Mission, assumes, with equally selfless devotion, the role of his legendary predecessor Thomas Jackson in feeding, clothing and cleansing the hungry and the homeless. In a building that has replaced the bombed-out Assembly Hall in Mile End, once the headquarters of that eccentric campaigner against Vice and Drink, Frederick Charrington, the Kenward Trust houses a specialist residential unit for post-detoxification cases with counselling support. At the northern periphery of our area, in Bethnal Green, a derelict Mansford Street Church has been transformed by a dynamic Unitarian minister, Tony Cross, into a community centre, where a well-equipped Employment Training scheme for 18 youths now functions. Cross has formed a team of local unwaged youths as volunteers to decorate old people's rooms and help with other domestic chores, and initiated a project to erect all-purpose accommodation units nearby for homeless single-parent families. He is also an active pastoral Minister, perpetually on call for advice and help by local people, whatever their creed.

Last but not least the Rev. Kenneth Leech, an Anglican socialist, is now ensconced as Director of the Runnymede Trust in Princelet Street. Formerly Rector of St Matthew's Church, Bethnal Green, he has been actively engaged for nearly forty years in rehabilitating young drug addicts and the older meths drinkers of Spitalfields. In 1962 he worked in the Simonlight Shelter off Cable Street, originally a brothel which was converted into a refuge for the homeless. He has since aided the Bangladeshi Youth Movement by acquiring funds for them from the Christian Council of Churches. A fearless opponent of racism, he campaigns actively against the National Front, and recently stood as prime witness in a court case brought against them.

These are but some of the bold spirits who are combatting the return to the social aberrations that defiled this area more than a century ago.

Pressures of gentrification on all sides are rapidly chang-
ing people and topography. From his own practical experi-
ence Charlie Forman puts it succinctly:

> The war for land is coming from all sides. One front is pushing
> up from the Docklands, another is spreading from the City,
> and a third is trying to force a corridor down the Liverpool
> Street railway line by way of the Bishopsgate Goods Yard.
> (*Spitalfields: a battle for land*, p. 261)

Such remaining streets as housed generation after generation of East End workers' families have almost vanished,
and many sites have been transmogrified into bastions of
middle-class settlement. Yet defensive action by local folk,
Bengalis and others, sometimes by united effort, has had
considerable success. Of the 1,274 new rented accommodation units promised in 1976, 805 had been built by 1986.
From Petticoat Lane to Vallance Road, in the northern sector
of the Whitechapel Road, is 'an almost unbroken run of new
housing estates' (Forman) inhabited to a large extent by ex-
tenement dwellers with genuine East End roots.

So in Parfett Street, off the Commercial Road, the Bethnal
Green and East London Housing Association had secured
and renovated condemned flats (earmarked for demolition
under the Abercrombie slum-clearance plan as far back as
1944!), which were promptly bought up by the Bengali
Sylhet Housing Corporation with GLC support to offer them
for sale on the open market. In Cressy Houses, by Stepney
Green, old rented tenancies are holding their own against
the encroachment of private buyers. Through Whitechapel

Commercial Street and the refurbished Christ Church, Spitalfields.
Beyond, Fournier Street: on the corner the Ten Bells pub, which has
now resumed the use of its original name. To the right of Christ Church
is Itchy Park, now inaccessible from the road and to its former occupants.

Puma Court from Commercial Street. Traditionally appropriate lamp standards replace the concrete monstrosity that stood here in 1977: so it is particularly unfortunate that British Telecom have seen fit to remove the old-style telephone box and substitute instead one of their execrably designed telephone points. At the far end, a small business.

and Mile End established East Enders are fighting back!

As we move east along the Mile End Road we see that some historical continuity is preserved: by Trinity Almshouses (built in 1695, yesterday under charitable endowment for retired seamen, today under private ownership!), whose gates confront the statue of William Booth, erected on the 'holy' spot where he preached his first witness for the Salvation Army; by the commemorative plaque at No. 88 on a wall that once protected the house of Captain Cook. Wickhams, the great 1930s store which clothed two generations of East Enders by hire-purchase, still functions as a wholesale distributor of domestic goods. But old Spiegelhalter, the jewellers, founded in 1828, who refused to sell to make way for a uniformly built Wickhams (they had to build round it!) has gone.

The ABC cinema, which once housed Lusby's and the Paragon Music Hall, against which the fierce campaigner Frederick Charrington pronounced anathema, stands desolate. His father's brewery by Cephas Avenue (formerly St Peter's Road) is now a depot, and the splendid eighteenth-century frontage has been replaced by a dull homogeneous brick façade. The areas in which gentrification has traditionally held fast (around Tredegar Square in Bow, and parts of Beaumont Square and Stepney Green in Mile End) remain inviolate, though the latter still retain a strong rearguard of old East End working-class families.

During the last decade there have been vast changes in class and topography around Whitechapel and Mile End. But much of the past is inexorable, thanks to the persistence of dedicated men and women fighting to retain the best of that past, particularly in defence of those old East Enders who refuse to move – and have the moral right to stay.

Renovation in Fournier Street. Not much more than a decade ago similar houses in Elder Street narrowly escaped demolition; whatever one's views on gentrification, it must be to its credit that these houses are now being preserved and restored to something like their original condition.

The Fournier Street backs, looking west. In the upper storeys some of the variations in the windows mark their former use as workrooms and sweatshops. Above the chimneys, the top of Christ Church spire.

A Fournier Street courtyard. Discovered by chance, this could be the Paris of the XIVme or XXme arrondissement before development swept it away. All that is lacking, *au fond de la cour*, is the proliferation of small trades.

Inside the courtyard. Above, the decaying roof of a one-time dairy: beyond, the lower storey of a beautifully restored eighteenth-century house, in the heart of Spitalfields yet invisible from any street.

Once Fournier Street was filled with small businesses plying the district's traditional trades:
now, in what has become a largely residential street, this one is relatively isolated.

Durward Street, formerly Bucks Row: Essex Wharf, the last surviving Ripper site, recorded one hundred years after the event. Across the street, a few feet from the further gateway, the body of Polly Nichols (generally regarded as the murderer's first victim) was found early in the morning on 31 August 1888. Not much prospect of a bicentennial shot.

Winthrop Street, desolated and abandoned, the ghost of a street, houses and inhabitants gone, no more than an echo of the vanishing Victorian East End. Only a derelict school and the cobbles remain.

Ford Square. To the right, public-sector housing, a corner shop at the far end: to the left, the beginning of the private sector, the division marked by a setback from the pavement and decorative ironwork.

Cressy Place, Stepney, at the height of the property boom.

Fieldgate Street. To the left, the synagogue: to the right, the crescent of Islam above the Whitechapel Mosque and the signboard of the Islamic Funeral Service symbolise a later immigration.

Settles Street, still in the main a haven for the trades which have flourished in East London since immigration began. For every legitimate firm operating there is probably an incalculable number of unlicensed and illegal workshops, ill-ventilated and with overloaded and near-lethal wiring.

Parfett Street. Dingy and decayed until recently, now sympathetically restored by the Bethnal Green and East London housing association. Centre, in the distance, the Fieldgate Street doss-house, patronised in 1907 by Joseph Stalin.

Wentworth Dwellings, Goulston Street. The Ripper passed this way on 30 September 1888 after the murder (his second that night) of Catherine Eddowes in Mitre Square. On the wall inside one of the entrances (now masked with corrugated iron) he almost certainly chalked the cryptic message 'The Juwes are The men That will not be Blamed for nothing'. A blood-stained piece of the victim's apron was found nearby. The buildings, though largely derelict and presumably due for demolition, are virtually unchanged.

Brick Lane: the new Spitalfields health centre, the Frying Pan pub (where Jack London used to drink when he was working on *People of the Abyss* in 1902) beyond. Compare this with the shot on p. 20 of *Streets of East London*.

Wentworth Street, and the former front entrance to Wentworth Dwellings. It is early morning, and the stallholders are just setting up for the day's trading. Here as perhaps nowhere else can one sense the atmosphere of nineteenth-century East London: but much of the area must be under threat, there cannot be long to go.

The mosque, Whitechapel Road. Services are relayed to the Jamme Mashid mosque, formerly the great synagogue, in Brick Lane.

Continuity in Brune Street : a Jewish business, established 1877, still trading.

Brune Street: the Jewish soup kitchen, maybe a touch shabbier than when photographed twelve years ago for *Streets of East London*, a few more windows broken: but still functioning.

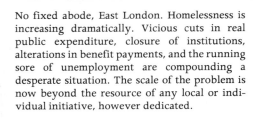

No fixed abode, East London. Homelessness is increasing dramatically. Vicious cuts in real public expenditure, closure of institutions, alterations in benefit payments, and the running sore of unemployment are compounding a desperate situation. The scale of the problem is now beyond the resource of any local or individual initiative, however dedicated.

Bengali brother and sister in the Chicksand Estate.

Mid-morning in Whitechapel. They have stopped for a chat; the dog has joined them.

They have emerged from Fieldgate Street and are heading towards the Whitechapel Road and Brick Lane. It is spring 1989. Looking for Salman Rushdie?

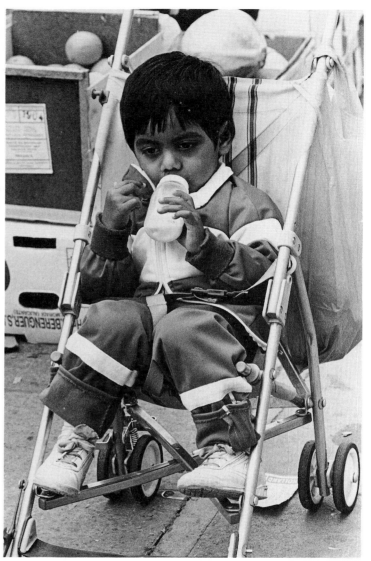

Local in a Fournier Street doorway.

In the Mile End Road, concerned only with essentials, and oblivious to the noise around him. The trousers have clearly been bought with an eye to the future.

Community wall art behind Christ Church, Spitalfields.

Trading in the Whitechapel Road. It is high summer, around midday, and the temperature is somewhere in the eighties.

Street-market shoppers in the Whitechapel Road.

Along the Mile End Waste.

Fieldgate Mansions. The uncompromisingly grim graffiti-covered red brick of the turn of the century tenement will never submit gracefully to improvement. The child's face, watchful and streetwise, could be peering from a doorway in any inner city – London, Liverpool, New York, Naples, Palermo.

In Commercial Street: an old local industry surviving.

Children's playground in Vallance Road.

Off Pedley Street: an old local industry revived.

The horse is grazing peacefully within a stone's throw of Brick Lane. A vital open space imaginatively located.

The Providence Row night shelter, Crispin Street, Spitalfields. For over a century it has dispensed comfort to the needy, the deprived, the desperate, the down and out: charity in the truest sense. There is no present sign that the economic miracle will make it redundant.

Foraging in Commercial Street, but with a difference: the proceeds are being loaded into the open back of the van on the right, destination unknown.

Spitalfields Market, 5–6 a.m. It is inevitable, given the intolerable pressure of traffic upon London, that the viability of central markets such as Spitalfields is being questioned. Even so, it brings needed employment to what is still in the main a chronically impoverished community : and if it is replaced it should be with something that offers more local opportunity than the usual arid office complex.

Spitalfields Market, 5–6 a.m.

Spitalfields Market, 5–6 a.m.

DOCKLANDS

by John M. Hall

Docklands as a title does not sit to happily in a book which follows on an earlier volume about the *streets* of East London, because it is not really an area of typical inner city streets. It is a disjointed area of massive civil engineering works – the docks, wharves, warehouses and paraphernalia of port and river-related industries – once intimately bound up with the River Thames which snakes along its flat flood-plain towards its estuary and the North Sea. Proper streets with houses were penned in between dock walls, factories, railway lines, gas works, timber yards: a chaotic clutter from the physical expansion of nineteenth-century London. And you cannot really grasp its scale either as the former home of the Port of London, or as what advertisements have claimed as Europe's largest single urban redevelopment project, from the street. You need to see it from the Thames on a river launch, preferably one pushing against a flood tide, so as to get a hint of the seamanship required to reach and sail away from the former docks.

Or if you are a senior politician you can fly over it in a helicopter. It was by this means that the term Docklands was coined. Peter Walker, Secretary of State for the Environment in 1971, got such a view. He made the mental leap, reserved in earlier generations for map-loving geographers, of linking together both banks of the Thames, and he called the area of 2,000 hectares (5,000 acres, or some 10 square miles) downstream from Tower Bridge and the

Tower of London 'the London Docklands'. Londoners, by contrast, would have told him that the river (hardly *their* river: who sees it, who uses it?) is a divide: even dockers would rarely cross the water to work on the other side.

The reason for identifying the London Docklands in 1971 as an area for comprehensive study of the potential for redevelopment was that since 1967 the upstream docks operated by the Port of London Authority had begun to close down. A mixture of reasons can be given: technological change, including the shift to roll-on/roll-off ferries; European and channel port competition as short sea traffic usurped the deep sea trade; trades union intransigence, and weak Port of London Authority management.

The closures were sudden: East India Docks in 1967; the London and St Katharine's Docks in 1968–69; the Surrey Commercial Docks on the south side in 1970. I like to call the docks in Wapping and the Surrey Docks the 'near east': close to the City of London whose enlarging role in controlling world seaborne trade generated the demand for enclosed docks to handle cargoes on the congested and tidal river Thames. As the twentieth-century City of London turned more to handling invisible items – titles to goods and services for the owners of goods such as insurance – so the demand for office space grew at the expense of former warehousing space, and Docklands is now viewed in part as easily accessible land suitable for accommodating overspill offices from the congested City of London. The fact that the office property market is also tidal, although the word cyclical is more commonly used, is one irony that might strike those of historical bent. The extent to which City-like functions can be lured to the middle east (the Isle of Dogs, where the West India and Millwall Docks closed in 1980), and the far east (the Royal Docks in Newham, closed in 1981), emerges later in this narrative.

So the 1970s opened with the new definition of Docklands as an area of opportunity for physical redevelopment on a vast scale. The dominant planning philosophy then was what has been dubbed 'needs-based planning'. In the Docklands context, this involved using the sudden windfall of vacant docks, warehouses, sidings and parking aprons, hitherto not properly integrated into the surrounding urban fabric, to build public housing in those East London boroughs seemingly predestined always to be impoverished by whatever measurements of poverty and deprivation are current. New factories would open to provide work for redundant dockers. Maybe a few offices would be attracted. Certainly new public transport services and road improvements would make the area get-at-able for employees and get-out-able for residents. (At the time, the Isle of Dogs was as far in travel time terms from, say, Trafalgar Square as Harrow, although only a quarter of the distance away.)

Such needs-based planning was firmly accepted by the three tiers of government which then had a direct interest in the future of the Docklands: central government (Labour from 1974–79), regional government, if we can call the Greater London Council that (Labour 1973–77), and the five solidly Labour East London boroughs of Tower Hamlets and Newham on the north bank, and Southwark, Lewisham and Greenwich on the south. I emphasise *government*, for another basic tenet was that redevelopment would be public-sector led and funded. But no sooner had an ambitious master plan been published (the London Docklands Strategic Plan of 1976), than the national economy had one of its periodic nasty turns, and public spending was squeezed. Nevertheless, the boroughs and the GLC had started to work together through a specially formed Docklands Joint Committee (DJC), which paid careful attention to developing fashions in public participation, and linked physical planning with programme management

But the moderately cosy relationship of Labour authorities in the home of some of the most notable battles on the warpath map of British socialism (the match-girls' strike of 1888, the dockers' tanner of the following year, the rise of Poplarism to dispense rates to the poor in the 1920s – the litany is properly covered in *The Streets of East London*) was soon to be challenged by the election of Margaret Thatcher as Conservative prime minister in 1979. Her new environment secretary, Michael Heseltine, also took the synoptic, bird's-eye view. He also viewed the tri-partite DJC as a hindrance to the effective regeneration (new word) of the area. From now on, the private sector would lead and fund, outweighing public sector investment by a ratio of 5:1 (almost the exact reverse of the balance of the mid-1970s, and itself rapidly improved upon as land values shot up). We were now in the era of 'demand-led planning', or, to use a once popular lyric: Que sera, sera – whatever will be, will be.

A new vision brought proposals for a new controlling structure. Two single-minded urban development corporations would be established, one to oversee the physical

DOCKLANDS

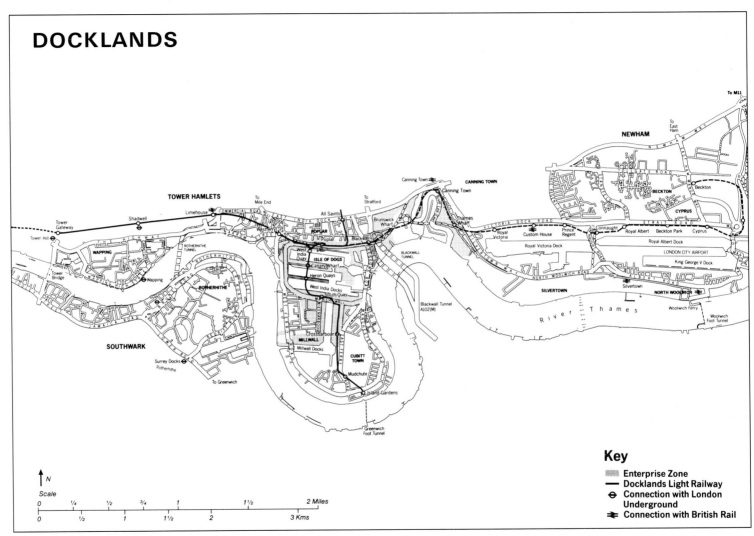

Key

- ▨ Enterprise Zone
- ▬ Docklands Light Railway
- ⊖ Connection with London Underground
- ⇌ Connection with British Rail

reproduced by courtesy of the LDDC.

regeneration of the London Docklands, and the other the similarly dedockised (for the *Oxford English Dictionary* admits of the word) Merseyside dock area. Such agencies would be modelled on the British new town development corporations. Within a designated area they have had powers to draw up a master plan, acquire land and, with government funding, build a 'balanced community' enjoying a full social, industrial and commercial life. Five peers sitting to hear several million words from petitioners in the House of Lords eventually agreed that London should have its development corporation, and in summer 1981 the London Docklands Development Corporation (LDDC) sprang into life. Its aim, as given in its most recent (1989) corporate plan, is 'to secure the lasting physical, economic and social regeneration of the urban development area'. Nicholas Breach's photographs capture the recent deeds more readily than the words of justification.

When a full history of the LDDC comes to be written it will have to be heavily biographical. Michael Heseltine appointed as chairman of the LDDC Nigel Broackes (later knighted), chairman of Trafalgar House, a company which occupies several pages of *Who owns whom* listings, and Bob Mellish (later ennobled) as his deputy. The chief executive until 1986 was Reg Ward, a model for the recruiters' advertisement phrases of self-starter and achiever. His swashbuckling approach caused periodic difficulties with Department of the Environment officials, but he delivered the goods: principally the turnaround from unwanted

Inside the Royal Victoria Dock, looking west. It opened for business in 1855 on land acquired at little more than the going agricultural rate. By 1860 it was handling double the tonnage of the London Docks: now grass and weeds grow in the crevices of the once thriving jetty.

derelict land and water in an unvisited part of London into desirable development sites by the Thames and dock waterfronts in a frequently televised, photographed and written about area.

The LDDC now lists six corporate aims. The first is improving access. This was crucial for Reg Ward and his small team of officers and part-time army of private sector consultants. He cajoled the staff into the deserted Olsen terminal in the Millwall Dock: 'If we don't get into Docklands, who will invest there?' was his question. In fact the Island (Isle of Dogs) became more than corporate headquarters site, it was the geographical and symbolic heart of the early regeneration effort. Geographical because of its centrality: middle east as I called it earlier. Symbolic because this is where the Docklands Light Railway, opened in 1987, was to run on its way to Island Gardens opposite the Royal Naval College in Greenwich, and where a 200-hectare (500-acre) enterprise zone was to be designated from 1982–92. Improving access – road and railway building – soon became the largest single item of expenditure in the LDDC's annual grant from the Treasury (about £70 million a year in the early 1980s), although compulsory land acquisition was most important in the first year, including buying up most of what was to become the enterprise zone from the previous owner, the Port of London Authority.

By 1990 improving access had come to include extending the DLR westwards to Bank underground station in the City of London (well under way), eastwards to Beckton once sanctioned by parliament, and indeed southwards to Lewisham. A public inquiry is to consider whether jet aircraft should be allowed to use the London City Airport, known when on the drawing board as the STOLport (short take-off and landing). Since it opened in 1987 on the finger of hard standing between the Royal Albert and King George V docks it has operated turbo-propeller aircraft on flights to Amsterdam, Brussels and Paris. By 1989 the momentum behind the emerging one million square metre Canary Wharf development on just 25 hectares of the West India Dock (see the cranescape on p. 90) caused the transport secretary to approve an extension of London's Jubilee underground line from Green Park and Westminster via Waterloo, London Bridge and Canary Wharf to Stratford in East London. One reason for approving this line, and the alignment through Canary Wharf, was Olympia and York's willingness to subscribe £400 million to the cost of the new underground. But surely, said some critics, the developers have enjoyed enormous tax concessions already by virtue of their enterprise zone site (including freedom from business rates until 1992, and 100 per cent reductions in liability for corporation tax): why does this entitle them to become London's de facto strategic transport planning authority?

That such an amount of construction activity as illustrated in this volume has been witnessed since the LDDC was created is proof that the second corporate aim, building confidence, has been realised. But was it by chance or design that in 1988, the year when the commercial and residential property markets in London began to shiver after five years of uninterrupted growth, the LDDC appointed a marketing directorate 'to create an enduring identity and image for London Docklands which is attractive to investors, businesses, employees, residents and decision-makers'? The LDDC's board and officers, hitherto upbeat and bullish, to use eighties' terminology, had to admit that it was proving difficult to maintain the development momentum in the far east especially. Newcomers to the rapidly appearing flats, suites, penthouses and town houses in Wapping, the Isle of Dogs and Surrey Docks, many of whom had bought for investment appreciation rather than habitation, were dismayed when the market shivered.

Another aim is encouraging investment. The LDDC's own words read like a Mars-bar advertisement, making the area 'pleasant and stimulating to live, work and play in'. Those recent immigrants to Wapping will not be aware of the historical social gradations between Wapping and Shadwell, even along particular streets. They will not plug in immediately to the intricate network of back-street suppliers and repairers of this and that; they will want superstore convenience, yellow pages quotations, choice and quality in shops, schools, restaurants or whatever. As newcomers in the 1980s they have paid the price for pioneering familiar to all new town residents: a feeling of living on a building site, waiting for Marks & Spencer to decide it is worth opening a store. In fact, M & S is committed to opening a store within the Canary Wharf office development: a real sign that that particular scheme is maturing according to its owners' vision. As for play, Docklands has been slow to see new leisure and sporting pastimes provided. An exception is the London Arena, adjacent to the LDDC's original Millwall Dock offices, which has offered indoor sports spectacles (American football, of course) and rock and pop groups (although the music critics carped about the problems of finding the place – Docklands is not properly on everybody's London street map yet).

It is when we look at another aim, that of generating jobs, that the jury remains out. In its own defence, the LDDC would say that their primary role was to stimulate regenera-tion, to encourage firms to set up in the area. Unfortunately for them, even after they began work, the toll of local unemployment went on rising, with rates for men approaching 30 per cent in what had become reduced to three Docklands boroughs in the mid-1980s. What became clear was that the new jobs attracted were bringing their workers with them from elsewhere in London – as in the case of newspaper printers from Fleet Street (although transfers led to widespread shedding of labour) – and certainly not soaking up the reserve army of local unemployed school-leavers and longer-term adult unemployed. Various enquiries were undertaken to examine the phenomenon further, and the House of Commons Employment Committee sought reassurance that more realistic targets would be set for reducing unemployment and training local school-leavers and adults to take advantage of the incoming industries, especially those in the high-tech and financial services sectors. So by the early 1990s there is increased emphasis on training, whether by colleges, firms, industrial sectors such as construction and catering, and by partnerships such as the much-copied East London schools-business partnership or 'compact'. The LDDC anticipates jobs within its boundary rising three-fold between 1987–88 (35,000 or so) to 115,000 by 1992–93. Less caution attaches to their estimates of completed new housing: 10,000 by 1988, another 10,000 by 1992–93. As a consequence the residential population of Docklands could rise to over 100,000 by the late 1990s, compared with 39,000 at the time of the 1981 census.

And what does all of this effort add up to? The grand aim is lasting regeneration: 'to ensure that all people living and working in the [Docklands] are able to take advantage of the opportunities created by regeneration and to establish

Security 1988: steel fencing and razor wire surround a site in the London Docks.

self-sustaining communities.' Some local critics would say, in mocking tones, that self-sustaining communities had been wilfully destroyed by the blight of successive planning pro-posals, by the construction itself, and by the deliberate overlaying of whatever is profitable on an area of severe social and environmental disadvantage. Certainly groups such as the Docklands Forum, local action groups, and the Newham 'people's plan' federation have demanded alterna-tive corporate aims angled more at those presently living, working or unemployed there, in preference to the socially mobile young people and geographically mobile tax-minimising firms sought by the LDDC. An analysis in this mould resurrects class conflict, the circuit of capital, and the language of earlier workers' struggles in the area.

It is interesting to see how the local Labour councils (although Tower Hamlets went Liberal in 1986 and also introduced decentralised administration) have fought, acquiesced in or supported the advent of private-sector led development. Broadly speaking, Tower Hamlets was the first to go native, Newham more cautious, and Southwark most vigorous in its opposition to the Conservatives' vision of Docklands' future. In part this results from the position of councils along a scale from left to left of left, in part to the property market fundamentals of near/middle/far east in terms of distance from the City of London.

How you view Docklands (and please *do* view it if you can: the photographs are to whet your appetite) depends on whether you are established resident or newcomer, old or young, employed or unemployed, at school, subject to or insulated from the construction frenzy, and so on. If you are a member of the Conservative government you will visit it to be photographed as often as possible, for this is the

North-eastwards in Bow Creek, Goliath from Manchester tied up at Jubilee Wharf.

regeneration model for other 'inner cities'. Unfortunately, few other development corporations or enterprise zones have had the advantage of such international attention. National Labour politicians have been somewhat less clamorous of late about their views on opportunities lost or bungled, but there is still plenty of uninhibited local criticism. It focuses on issues of who pays, who gains and who loses, whether using macro-economic arguments about the globalisation of production and investment, and tax liabilities, or detailed studies of individuals and households which may show little evidence of the new-found wealth rapidly trickling down to Docklands residents or those in the adjacent East London boroughs.

In summary, the Docklands experiment is not directly transportable to other places. Where else were there over 20 million cubic metres of idle impounded water so close to the financial heart of the national capital? Where else is central government willing to put in such a volume of public funding to prime the pump and woo private capital – and to back up money with powers, influential leadership and entrepreneurial talent? Where else, indeed, can there have been such a breathtaking onslaught by the enterprise culture on the expiring stronghold of municipal socialism, trades union power, and the obsolete physical monuments to the sometime supremacy of the United Kingdom in maritime trade? I have been captivated by the damp romance of the Docklands waterfront for twenty years or more: do come along by Docklands Light Railway, bus, car or bike to see for yourself. It is too large to walk around except in separate excursions. And do not overlook the main Docklands high street, the River Thames itself.

Getting around

Visitors to London with only a short time to spend should certainly combine both a trip on the River Thames from Westminster/Charing Cross/Tower Pier to Greenwich with a trip on the Docklands Light Railway from Tower Gateway to Island Gardens. It matters little which is used for the outward journey, which for the inward.

For those with time to walk, there are north and south bank routes. On the north bank, walk from Tower Hill underground station via St Katharine's Dock to Wapping underground station, or even to Limehouse and the DLR or bus if time permits. On the south bank, walk from London Bridge underground station along the waterfront to the Design Museum and thence to Rotherhithe underground station. Each route can be done in reverse, of course, but requires a street atlas, of which there are several, or one of the new Docklands maps.

For those travelling by car, minibus or coach there is the possibility of a half-day excursion taking in Wapping, the Isle of Dogs and the foot tunnel from Island Gardens to Greenwich (a suitable lunch stop), or a complete circuit of Docklands in a full day.

The full day allows a tour of the South Bank, from London Bridge to the Surrey Docks, lunch at Greenwich, Thames Barrier visitor centre, Woolwich Ferry (if running; otherwise the short-circuit via the Blackwall Tunnel), North Woolwich, Beckton (take the footpath to the top of the ski slope for the panorama), and returning via London City Airport, Leamouth, the Isle of Dogs (enterprise zone and Canary Wharf), Wapping and thence to St Katharine's Dock and the City of London.

Bus services have been much improved, and allow reasonable connections with central London, although anticipate delays from traffic jams. Generally the Docklands Light Railway is the best way of travelling on the north bank, although it might be closed at weekends for major upgrading.

Across the Royal Victoria Dock from Silvertown Way. The gap in the group of tower blocks to the left marks the former site of Ronan Point, demolished after a gas explosion in 1968 caused a partial collapse.

Progress shot in the Millwall Dock, framed by the gothic arch of an abandoned crane. The project is now complete.

The Gallions Hotel near the Albert Dock, haven for generations of sailors. Isolated and abandoned, it could be the shuttered and decaying wreck of some forgotten Edwardian magnate's mansion.

Wapping Old Stairs and the Town of Ramsgate. Both are survivors: the river stairs are vanishing fast, and the riverside pubs (Arthur Morrison's eponymous *Hole in the Wall* was located in Wapping) have all but disappeared.

Oliver's Wharf from St John's Churchyard, the first of the warehouse conversions.

Death of a pub: the Turk's Head in Scandrett Street, Wapping. Wine bars and brasseries are more in keeping with the new dockland image.

The last of Nesham Street.

Eastwards across the London Docks. For some inscrutable reason new buildings have been made to masquerade as warehouse conversions, an irritating architectural sophism. The shot was taken from Nesham Street, a derelict roadway marked on no map, and now obliterated completely.

The London Docks in 1977: towards Pennington Street and Ratcliffe.

The London Docks in 1977: west towards St Katharine's.

From Discovery Walk, behind Tench Street, across the Western Dock. The tower of St George's-in-the-East locates the Ratcliffe Highway, once one of the East End's most dangerous streets and now dangerous only to cross.

Spirit Quay in the Western Dock, lifeless as a model, without shops, cafés, pubs, lacking everything that makes a community.

Housing in Discovery Walk.

Tower Bridge, the logo of the London Docklands Development Corporation. In 1952 Pevsner wrote: 'the massive structure does much damage to the skyline of the City and the apparent scale of the Tower' (*The Buildings of England*, London, vol. II). Would that he were still with us to comment on Canary Wharf.

Community association poster near the Rotherhithe tunnel.

Community association poster, Isle of Dogs.

Narrow Street: once the entrance to the Regent's Canal Dock, long since blocked. Opened in 1820, it provided a link, via the Grand Junction Canal at Paddington, with the industrial Midlands. The staple cargo was coal.

Crumbling dockland housing in Narrow Street. It was just the same in 1977, and had amazingly survived, undemolished, for over a decade. But the bulldozers were just round the corner, and shortly after this shot was taken they moved in.

From the Limehouse shore to the Isle of Dogs. Dark skies over a dead river.

Isle of Dogs: warehousing in Cuba Street. Sound and traditional with a human dimension, but short-term lets only.

Agent's board, Burrell's Wharf, Isle of Dogs. It is spring '88 and property is appreciating by the day. At these prices, not many local buyers: but the financial climate has grown colder since, and some of Kentish's subsequent projects have been less than successful.

The Docklands Light Railway and the perspex cupola of the Island Gardens terminus.

From the platform across Cubitt Town towards Blackwall.

Isle of Dogs. Original cottages sandwiched between a modern development and, on the far left, self-built houses of some years ago.

Poplar High Street: in the foreground, site of the Poplar workhouse, mentioned by Jack London in *People of the Abyss*, 1903. The nearby technical college, though much altered, looks as though it could have been part of the original complex.

Spillers Millennium Mills in the Victoria Dock, an impressive group that deserves to be listed;
though these days in docklands – or indeed anywhere – listing is no guarantee of preservation.

Office of the Poplar Labour Party, so often in the forefront of the fight for social justice in East London. Closed: but hopefully for the day only.

Temple of the Filofax : the former wine vaults beneath Tobacco Dock.

From Connaught Road, Silvertown, summer 1988: development at the eastern end of the Victoria Dock. Centre, the CWS building, begun in 1938, still solid and confident amid the surrounding desolation. In 1940 Silvertown took the full ferocity of the Luftwaffe's attack on dockland.

Bow Creek from Leamouth Road, much of it still undisturbed, but the bulldozers are busy not far away in the East India Dock.

The enterprise zone, summer 1989. From Marsh Wall across the West India Dock towards Canary Wharf: the apotheosis of the crane.

The enterprise zone. Megalopolis.

Manilla Street, in the heart of the enterprise zone: an old-established local business in an improbably arcadian setting. Centre, a board advertises another local business.

A long-established scrapyard adjoining the barrier approach in Silvertown.

Across the West India Dock and the Isle of Dogs from Preston Road, with the enterprise zone to the left, Cascades, a weird high-tech Gormenghast, in the distance, and small yachts in the dock basin.

Eastwards from the walkway above Tower Bridge. In the foreground, the upper pool; centre,
in the distance, the cranes around Canary Wharf. The completed project could devastate
London's skyline.

BIBLIOGRAPHY

Ambrose, P., *Whatever Happened to Planning?* (Methuen, London, 1986)

Audit Commission, *Urban Regeneration and Economic Development: the local government dimension* (HMSO, London, 1989)

Broodbank, Sir Joseph, *History of the Port of London* (Daniel O'Connor, London, 1921)

Brown, R.D., *The Port of London* (Terence Dalton, Lavenham, Suffolk, 1978)

Church, A., 'Urban regeneration in the London Docklands', *Environment and Planning* C, 6 (1988), 187–208

Church, A. and Hall, J. M., 'Discovery of Docklands', *Geographical Magazine*, Vol. 58, No. 12 (1986), 632–40

Church, A. and Hall, J.M., 'Local initiatives for economic regeneration', in D.T. Herbert and D.M. Smith (ed), *Social Problems and the City* (OUP, Oxford, 1989), 345–69

Colquhoun, P., *Commerce and Police of the River Thames* (Joseph Mawman, London, 1800)

Cunningham, P., *Handbook for London* (John Murray, London, 1849)

Docklands Consultative Committee, *Urban Development Corporations: six years in London's Docklands* (DCC, 1988)

Docklands Joint Committee, *London Docklands Strategic Plan* (GLC, London, 1976)

Employment Committee, House of Commons, *The Employment Effects of Urban Development Corporations* (Third Report, Session 1987–88; HC 327-I; HMSO, London, 1988)

Fishman, W.J. and Breach, N., *Streets of East London* (Duckworth, London, 1979)

Forman, C., *Spitalfields: a battle for land* (Shipman, London, 1989)

Hall, J.M., *Metropolis Now: London and its region* (CUP, Cambridge, 1990)

Hatton, E., *A New View of London* (Chiswell, London, 1708)

Hill, S., *The Dockers: class and tradition in London* (Heinemann, London, 1976)

Hughson, D., *Walks through London* (Sherwood, Neely, London, 1841)

Knight, C. (ed), *London* (6 vols) (Knight, London, 1841/4)

Leech, K., *Brick Lane 1978: the events and their significance* (Affor, Birmingham, 1978)

London, J., *The People of the Abyss* (Isbister, London, 1903)

London Docklands Development Corporation, latest issue of the annual *Corporate Plan* and *Annual Report and Accounts*

Mayhew, H., *London Labour and the London Poor* (Griffin & Bohn, London 1861/2)

National Audit Office, *Department of the Environment: Urban Development Corporations* (HC 492; HMSO, London, 1988)

North East London Polytechnic, *Dockland: an illustrated historical survey of life and work in East London* (Thames & Hudson, London, 1986)

Palmer, A., *The East End: four centuries of London life* (John Murray, London, 1989)

Pevsner, Sir Nikolaus, *The Buildings of England, London I/II* (Penguin, London, 1973)

Public Accounts Committee, House of Commons, *Urban Development Corporations* (Twentieth Report, Session 1988–89; HC 385, HMSO, 1989)

Pudney, J., *London's Docks* (Thames & Hudson, London, 1976)

Seymour, R., *Survey of the Cities of London & Westminster* (Read, London, 1734)

Ward, R., 'London: the emerging Docklands city', *Built Environment* 12 (1986), 114–27

Weale, J. (ed), *London and its Vicinity* (Weale, London, 1851)